GW00384778

ROCHE VILLAGE MEMORIES
by
C.R. EDYVEAN

© 1995 C.R. Edyvean

ISBN No: 0 902660 225

PUBLISHED BY THE FEDERATION OF OLD CORNWALL SOCIETIES

Printed by Palace Printers, Lostwithiel.

PREFACE

My interest started with Roche at an early age. I was christened at Roche Parish Church and both my parents are Roche people. My mother's side were the Oliver family who lived at Carbis and my father being Edyvean has one of the oldest names in the Roche parish register. My Grandmother left me a good collection of photographs and postcards of the village. This whetted my appetite to start this book. As a postman I delivered mail to a part of Roche and outlying farms etc. I have tried to keep this book simple, as Roche was covered by Cresswell Payne quite extensively in the late 1940's. I am also indebted to many people around the Roche area who have stimulated my interest in collecting old photographs and memories of Roche.

ACKNOWLEDGEMENTS

I would like to express my appreciation and grateful thanks to the following for their help in the production of this book.

For information and for the use of their photographs.

My father, Ralph Edyvean.
My Aunt, Jean George.
Miss Eva Ward.
Mr. John Tonkin.
Mr. Ivan Trevenna.

For their encouragement to complete this historic and photographic record of Roche.

My wife, Marilyn.
Valerie Brokenshire.

Robert Evans, Publications Officer of the Federation of Old Cornwall Societies and the Federation for their assistance in publishing this book.

C.R. Edyvean (Sam) - 1995
Trethurgy,
St. Austell,
Cornwall.

INTRODUCTION

Roche is situated fairly central in Cornwall, approximately 1,032ft above sea level. The village is 6 miles from St. Austell and about 8 miles from Bodmin. There are three rivers that start in the Roche parish. The River Fal which rises in Colvreath, the Par River which rises in Penstrase and a small stream that rises at Holy Well, flows into the River Camel.

One of the first things seen as you approach the village from the St. Austell side is the outcrop of rocks with its chapel perched precariously on the top. On the approach down the A30 you are met with the beautiful Goss Moor. To the right a high hill with an ancient hillfort on top, with a disused wolfram mine on the side, is Castle-an-Dinas. The Goss Moor was also streamed for tin in early years and later dredged. Approaching from the St. Dennis side of the village you pass Retillick Moor. Roche itself is surrounded by several hamlets, Carbis, Tregoss, Trezaise, Tremodrett and Belowda, or Belovely as called by some local people. The village itself has had a steady development over the years. The population for 1939 was 2,000, it is now 2,353 (recorded in 1991 census).

The main industry is now clay, but in the past there was a brickworks at nearby Carbis, a Glass Mine at Polpuff, tin on the Goss Moor, Wolfram at Castle-an-Dinas and a stone quarry at Trezaise (Glebe Quarry). Farming also played a major role in village life. The village is also served with a railway and had a station which is now reduced to a halt. This is the Par to Newquay branch line.

About one mile from Roche on the road to Demelza, turn right down a lane to Holy Well. This is a lovely little well which is said to be 14th century and had special healing properties in its water. It was restored in 1937 by St. Austell Old Cornwall Society. There are three inns in Roche, the Victoria on the A30, the Commercial (now named The Poachers) and the Rock Inn, both in Fore Street. Rock Inn is dated 1587.

The map below was in the book, The Story of the parish of Roche, by H.M. Creswell Payne.

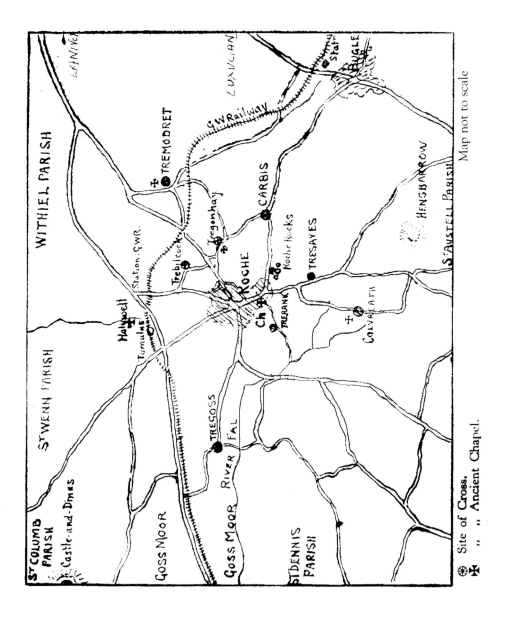

Map not to scale

Roche Church.

Roche Parish Church was named after St. Gomonda, who came to Roche as a missionary from Wales. The Norman church was built in 1100 A.D. and the tower was added in 1400 A.D. and rises to a height of 85ft. with a peal of eight bells and a clock. The font is made from Pentewan stone and dates from about 1180.

Many changes have been done to the church. The most drastic was by Rev. Fisher from 1820-22, when he gutted the inside walls. It was also changed again in 1890 by Rev. Thornton who changed the slate floor for a wood block one. The stained glass window was given by Mr. A. Bennetts of Sutton, Surrey on 27th December 1924, and depicts when Jesus was born.

Standing in the churchyard is a large wheel headed Cornish cross. There are two other Cornish crosses to be found in Roche, one in the Rectory field and the other on private land in the Old Rectory.

Roche. Church and Memorial.

Above: Photo taken by Ward of Roche in the early 1920's showing the gates in the church on the right before road widening. The gates are now on the left of the church.

Below: Photo taken in the 1940's now with telephone poles and the corner taken back where the monument stands. In recent times the letter box has been removed.

ROCHE, THE CHURCH.

Above: Interior of the church taken a few years ago when paraffin lamps were the only means of light.

Below: Roche bell ringers, the young and the old. This photo was taken on 4th March, 1948.
Left to Right are: Reg Hewitt, Wesley Kendall, Robert Camps, Jack Harris, ? Reg Brenton, Lenny Brenton, Harold Bennett, Orlando Benney.

Left: Pictured here is the monument to the 32 men who lost their lives in the First World War. Today the monument has the names of a further 8 men who lost their lives in the Second World War. Above the wall can be seen the top of the Rock.

Below: Cornwall Diocesan Pilgrimage. The Bishop of Truro, the Archdeacon of Bodmin, and Canons of the Cathedral Church heading the procession from the village schoolroom to Roche Rock.
August 1932

Above: This photograph shows the Unveiling and Dedication of the Roche War Memorial on the 16th March, 1921. The service was conducted by Parson Lowe.

Below: Armistice Day 11th November, 1921. The children attending the service with Miss Eva Ward placing a wreath on the memorial. Mr. Dempster the Headmaster is on the left.

Left: Grand Bard, Mr. H. Jenner speaking at the Gorsedd with the Rock in the background when the Gorsedd was held at Roche in 1933.

Bottom: The Bards walking down to the Rock for the ceremony.

Top: Gorsedd Ceremony in the shadow of the Rock.

Bottom: A Bard sounding the four blasts of the Corn Gwlas.
The Grand Bard (Mr. Henry Jenner) is seated immediately on the left of the trumpeter.

Roche Rock

Above: This photograph is by Ward of Roche and shows quite a lot of space between the Rock and church. Today with the trees grown up, the church is almost out of sight and the small rocks are almost covered by vearns (ferns).

Left: The size of the chapel window is shown by the boys. This photograph was taken by Ellis of Bodmin in 1941.

East Window, Chapel Ruins, Roche Rock, Cornwall.

Roche Rock and Bogle Road.

Two views taken from the church tower. The top one showing cows rambling down towards Carbis in the middle of the road. The photograph below looks down Rock Hill and most of the village.

Roche from Church Tower.

Holy Well Roche

This 15th century holy well lies about 1½ miles from Roche north of the A30. It was once used by miners for their water and also as a wishing well. Young unmarried girls from Roche used to throw pins and needles into the well and from the brightness of the bubbles tried to discover their good or bad fortune.

Below: Trezaise. This view looking from Roche is now part of Roche football field.

These photographs show the Ancient Order of Foresters Friendly Society.

Above: Taken in the Rectory field with the Rock Inn in the background. The man on the right holding the banner is Mr. Ward, a photographer who lived in Roche. The man sitting in the front row, 2nd right is George Edyvean, my Grandfather. He joined the Society on the 30th October, 1899.

Below: Carnival procession coming down Roche hill with the Foresters carrying the banner in the background.
The meeting place for the Society was the Temperance Hall which is at the crossroads in the centre of the village. It was listed as Lodge No. 270.

Both photographs show the villagers getting ready to go on a Sunday School trip. The top photograph was taken at the bottom of Roche Hill outside the Old Rectory and the bottom photograph was taken at the crossroads of Harmony Road and the Temperance Hall.

Above: William John Jolly's ice cream cart. He lived in Edgecumbe Terrace.

Below: Carnival Day. This photograph shows Billy Kendall standing with his race horses. Nelson Edyvean is one rider and the lady is Nella Penny.

Above: All dressed up in their Sunday best sitting in a beautiful pony and trap. This photograph was taken in Duck Street (Tremodrett Road) around the turn of the century.

Below: Little has changed since this photograph was taken of Tremodrett Road.

Top: The first covered-in bus to come into Roche, approx. 1926, called the Princess. It is stopped outside the Old Rectory, with my grandfather, Charles Oliver, sitting in the front passenger seat.

Below: Mr. Sleeman with his milk lorry parked outside Pitsmingle bungalow.

Both of these photographs are looking up Edgecumbe Road. By the children's dress and the rough surface of the roads I would think these were taken around the early part of the century.

Above: Taken in the mid 1930's on the right is Marcus Trethewey's Garage. The row of cottages has been demolished to make way for a bungalow now standing on the site.

Below: Shows the Temperance Hall, erected in 1884. It could seat 250 people and was a memorial to the Reverend Thomas Pearce. It was later used as a Working Men's Institute, then a Judo Club and now an auction room. On the other side of the road was Mrs. Cotton's shop.

Above: This postcard sent in 1910 shows the Fore Street with S.P. Ward's house (local photographer) first left.

Below: The same scene today. Little has changed except for a better road and the many electric and telephone wires.

Above: This lovely photograph with the girls in the front was taken on the corner of Duck Street (Tremodrett Road) to Fore Street. The shop at the far end was Norman Hawkey's Butcher Shop and the little shop on the left was a milliners shop owned by Miss. Moyses and Mrs. Lawrey.

Below: The same road as it is today. The shop and cottages on the left having been demolished.

Above: Edgecumbe Road showing the Terrace and the horse drawn butchers van. Roche was a much quieter place in those days.

Below: The Hawkey family taken outside Trerank farmhouse in about 1911. The house and porch has changed very little over the years and is virtually the same today.

Mothers' Union at Roche - These photographs were both taken in the Rectory field. The Rev. J.T. Tarplee is in the top photograph who was Rector for 26 years and retired in 1948. On his retirement he was presented with a cheque by Mr. Dempster who was the Headmaster of Roche School. The money was collected by the parishioners and Mrs. Tarplee was presented with a handbag. Photographs taken in 1948.

Top: I am not certain what the occasion was but it took place outside the Old Rectory about the turn of the century. My Grandmother, Mrs. Edyvean, nee Mary Phillipps, is standing on the far right. This photograph was taken by Mr. Ward, a photographer who lived in Roche.

Below: This fine photograph was taken outside the Old Rectory. The lady and gentleman in the front are Parson Lowe and his wife.

Above: Roche schoolgirls' netball team. The teacher is Miss Stickland. The game is being played in a field on the side of Duck Street (Tremodrett Road).

Below: Photograph taken outside the chapel in Tremodrett. This is believed to be a Bible Christian gathering.

Extracts from Roche School - Infant Log Book

Thursday, 27th August, 1874
School unswept which makes much against the proper discipline of the school.

29th October, 1874
Children had holiday given them this afternoon on account of the Audit of the school accounts.

Friday, 7th May, 1875
Stone picking has kept away some children from school this week.

10th April, 1876
Holiday this afternoon that the room may be cleaned.

20th June, 1876
Holiday in consequence of thje opening of the C.M. Railway. All the children at the request of the Board walked in procession to the Station headed by a band of music and were presented with a bun.

11th August, 1876
Drinking cans have been introduced this week.

26th June, 1877
Holiday in consequence of the Bishop of Truro being here to consecrate the piece of ground added to the Churchyard.

30th January, 1880
The fixing of the school bell has had the effect of making the attendance more punctual in coming to school as the excuse of not knowing the time is to a great extent done away with.

13th February, 1880
Half-holiday this afternoon on account of the men putting up the porch in the room, the hammering etc. being a great annoyance.

29th May, 1882
Holiday being Whit-Monday and the corner stone of the new Temperance Hall laid.

29th February, 1884
Half-holiday yesterday in consequence of the public tea for opening Organ at the Church being held in the schools.

19th September, 1884
We have suffered no small inconvenience for many months through failure on the part of someone to put up the school blinds to the windows. I have persistently reported the matter to the School Board but no improvement is seen, and children and teachers are broiled.

1st May, 1885
The children had holiday yesterday afternoon so that we might attend the funeral of the Rev. R.F. Gardiner, a member of the School Board.

21st June, 1887
Holiday today on account of a Festival being held for the Queen's Jubilee.

8th July, 1887
We had holiday on Monday on account of the wild beasts being in the village.

1st November, 1887
School closed for 4 weeks on account of an epidemic of diphtheria.

4th - 18th May, 1888
Board met on Monday and decided to make an alteration in the mode of collecting the school fees. In future all who have not brought their money by Tuesday are to be sent home.

6th - 10th August, 1888
Closed School on Monday (Bank Holiday) as there was a bazaar at the Rock. Wretched attendance the rest of the week. The people grudge paying 2d. for 4 days schooling, and always keep their children home if we have a whole or half holiday.

Tuesday, 10th March, 1891
Not a single child has put in an appearance today. A snow storm is raging. It began yesterday afternoon. The roads are all blocked, so shall close school this week. There is a large drift of snow in our yard just in front of the school door about a dozen feet high and a similar one in front of the Infant School door.

11th March, 1891
The children had holiday on Wednesday on account of Bostock's Menagerie being in the village.

11th April, 1892
Commenced Penny Bank today, 21 children deposited 8/6d. (42½p) which I consider a very fair beginning.

16th December, 1895
The Infant School was held in the new schoolroom today.

1st June, 1897
School closed in the afternoon there being a circus in the place and an afternoon performance for children.

5th October, 1897
Yesterday and today the workmen have been building a chimney on the other side of the Infant School prior to setting up the new stove.

1st March, 1900
Owing to the news of the Relief of Ladysmith on 28th February reaching us today, the Chairman gave a half-holiday in honour of the event.

1st June, 1900
School closed this afternoon and for a fortnight in consequence of the measles by the Sanitary Authority. The school (after being closed for six weeks in consequence of sickness by order of the Sanitary Authority) re-opened this morning with very small numbers.

12th November, 1901
Terrific gale of wind and rain - only 40 children present this morning (150 absent) - some children very wet. Registers not marked.

2nd June, 1902
News of the signing of the Treaty of Peace between Briton and Boer reached here this morning. Children with the consent of the Board had a half holiday in the afternoon. One orange as remembrance of above was distributed to every child.

14th September, 1903
Took children in Stds IV - VII accompanied by teacher to Plymouth on Saturday and had a most enjoyable and instructive day.

Programme:-
Left Victoria at 7.43 am.
Arrived Saltash 9.30am. and took steamer down the Hamoaze to Mutton Cove.
Through Dockyard and then by electric tram to Plymouth.
Lunch on the Hoe.
Visited memorials there and then Mount Batten, Barbican, Guildhall, Market, Reservoir and Streets.
Left again at 6 pm. and got home safely at 8.30 pm.

19th November, 1903
Boys in Std. IV - VII had a paper chase today instead of Recreation and Drill.

31st May, 1907
School will be closed this afternoon so that the teachers may attend the Annual Meeting of the N.U.T. at Truro.

24th January, 1908
The Chairman having given his consent I have decided not to open school today as the flue is out of order, and we are unable to have fire.

28th July, 1908
A days holiday to be given tomorrow for Trezaise Band of Hope Outing.

12th July, 1909
School closed today for a fortnight on the authority of the Medical Officer.

20th May, 1910
This school will be closed on 20th Friday instant for the funeral of King Eward VII in obedience of the Royal Proclamation.

22nd February, 1911
School will be closed tomorrow for the re-opening of the Belfry.

2nd June, 1911
In obedience to the wishes of the King and Queen the school will be closed during Coronation Week.

5th October, 1911
The Challenge Shield for singing won at Bodmin at the County Competition in May last was presented to the children this afternoon. Quite an interesting function.

24th April, 1913
This school will be closed tomorrow to enable children and teachers to visit the St. Austell and St. Columb District Exhibition at St. Austell.

25th May, 1913
This school will be closed tomorrow to give teachers and children an opportunity of attending the Bath and West Show at Truro.

9th September, 1913
This school will be closed tomorrow as the use of the Mixed Department is required for the "Clay Workers Ballot".

8th February, 1915
Four Belgian Refugee children who are being accommodated in the parish were admitted this morning.

1st March, 1915
The workmen have commenced the alterations of the school premises.

17th March, 1916
For the four weeks ended today the children have brought 222 eggs for wounded soldiers in the hospitals.

27th September, 1916
Notification has been received from the Board of Education that this Roche Infant Department now provides accommodation for not more than 116 children.

1st November, 1916
The children have subscribed £1. 14s. 0d. (£1.70) to the "Daily News Christmas Pudding Fund" for our soldiers and sailors.

18th December, 1916
The children have sent as a second Christmas gift to the Overseas Club the sum of 9 shillings (45p).

25th January, 1917
A War Savings Association is being formed in connection with the school.

6th July, 1917
The school closes this evening for one week - time being given for the Hay Harvest.

25th October, 1918
Influenza is spreading among the children. School closed for 4 weeks.

30th July, 1919
A half-holiday is granted this afternoon having been won by children for amount raised for War Loan.

1st Augst, 1919
In accordance with the wishes of the King the County Authority has granted an extra week's holiday as a "Peace Holiday" - this extra week's holiday will be given at the close of the period previously fixed for summer vacation - therefore the holidays will be extended to 5 weeks.

16th March, 1921
A half-holiday is given this afternoon on account of the Unveiling and Dedication of Roche War Memorial.

27th May, 1921
As a fire broke out in the village last Tuesday at a wood store - the children went to see the fire-engine and men at work.

24th June, 1921
This school was closed yesterday - a holiday being given in remembrance of the visit to Cornwall of the Prince of Wales.

11th November, 1921
The children observed "Armistice Day" by assembling around the monument and there laying wreaths and singing hymns.

27th February, 1922
A whole holiday being granted tomorrow this school will be closed - according to H.M. The King having expressed a desire that all schools be closed on 28th February, the Wedding Day of H.R.H. Princess Mary.

15th July, 1922
Sir Robert Fossett's Circus is visiting Roche today and a half-holiday is given this afternoon to enable children to attend the afternoon performance.

25th April, 1933
Received circular letters from Education Office that this school must be closed tomorrow according to the wish to H.M. The King, that a whole holiday granted to all schools on the 26th instant the Wedding Day of H.R.H. The Duke of York.

21st July, 1925
School closed this afternoon on account of Roche Cherry Fair and Sports.

24th October, 1927
Mr. Dempster (Manager) paid a call to this school this afternoon to inform me that the children are requested to attend the opening ceremony of the new recreation ground on Tuesday next at 3pm.

14 th May, 1928
Received letter from District Clerk stating that the Cornwall Education Authority had sanctioned purchase of school piano and authorising payment for same. Paid Messrs. Moon & Sons, Plymouth the sum of £20 being the school contribution to cost of new piano.

15th December, 1928
Introduced a school badge taking form of the Roche Rock. Silver on black.

24th April, 1929
We have taken a motto for the school badge of the Rock. Also each House has its own motto. Mr. R. Morton Nance of Chylaron, Carbis Bay has kindly put them into old Cornish :-

School badge:-
Awos an Awel, whath y whraf sevel - "Despite the gale, yet I do stand"

Tregarrick:-
Mar gref avel an Garek - "As strong as the Rock"

Trenowth:-
Plegya a-yllyn, terry ny - vynnyn - "Blend we may, break we will not"

Tregothnan:-
Gwell yu Genen Gul es cows - "We prefer doing to speaking"

Tremodrett:-
Pup-Huny Rag Les An Myns - "Each one for the good of all".

19th June, 1929
School playing field pegged out by County Architect.

31st July, 1929
School field opened by Mr. F.R. Pascoe, Secretary for Education, who hauled up the school flag for the first time.

16th July, 1930
A burlesque of an ancient tournament.

15th January, 1931
Formation of Roche School Folk Dancing Society.

24th April, 1931
The Cooking Centre is working.

15th December, 1933
A half-holiday has been granted by the Cornwall Education Authority this afternoon to enable the teachers to attend the presentation ceremony at Truro for Mr. F.R. Pascoe.

1st November, 1934
Milk supply commenced.

28th November, 1934
A whole holiday is being given tomorrow - the wedding day of the Duke of Kent.

7th May, 1935
This school was closed yesterday for the Silver Jubilee.

27th January, 1936
Funeral of His late Majesty King George V.   The County Committee has decided to close all schools under their jurisdiction on that day, and that Head Teachers be asked to explain the purpose of the closure.

6th May, 1937
On Wednesday the King and Queen will be crowned in Westminster Abbey and you, the school children of England and Wales will be given a holiday in honour of that memorable event.

30th November, 1937
This school will be closed for the whole day tomorrow to commemorate the visit of His Majesty the King to Cornwall.

26th January, 1940
According to instructions given in a letter from County Hall all the children in this school have had their gas masks examined during the week. According to instructions received in the circular letter referring to Government Evacuation Scheme the double shift system commenced in this school today.

27th June, 1940
Commencing Monday 1st July the evacuated children should attend school in the morning and the local children in the afternoon, alternating week by week until further notice.

12th August, 1940
The children of the infant school will from today receive their instruction in the main classroom of the Mixed Department - the Infant School being used by the London evacuees.

Above: The girls look very cold in this school photograph
taken in the winter of 1923.

Below: Roche School 1920's. On the shield in the front can be seen the word
Tregothnan which was one of the school's house names.

Above: Roche Home Guard group photo taken by Ellis of Bodmin on 20th August, 1944. (From Cornish Studies Library, Redruth).

Below: Cornish Wrestling, the Stickler (Ref) seeing a proper hitch or throw is being carried out. Contestants are Chapman and Gregory. Photograph taken by Ellis from Cornish Studies Library.

Above: Roche Working Mens' Club Billiards Team, winners of the Mid Cornwall League Shield 1922-1923 season.
Back row left to right: *Williams, Dick Hocking, Dempster (Headmaster), Hancock and William Trethewey.*
Front row: *S.P. Ward, Bassett, Best and Tom Perry.*

Left: This photograph shows a St. Dennis man who wheeled 3 cwt. of cement up Roche Hill for a bet in 1927.

Billiards being played in the Roche Institute Room. In the top photograph is Bill Trethewey on the left and Rupert George on the right. In the bottom photograph is Jack Mitchell on the left and Rupert George on the right.

Both of these photographs show Roche Football Club. The top photograph in 1919-1920 season and the bottom photograph in the 1929-1930 season.

Top Photograph:
Back row: *Fred Dempster, Moss Marshall, ? Mel Gray, Len Burton, Parsons Lowe, John George.*
Middle row: *Martin Tonkin, Dan Bassett, Clar Richards, Bob Cock, ?*

Bottom Photograph
Back row: *Jack Hocking, George Burton, Morris Tonkin, Alf Oliver, Ralph Caddy, Moss Marshall, Harry Gregory. Middle row: Cecil Roberts, ?, ?*
Bottom row: *Ed Tonkin, ?, Hedley Vennor, Les Gill, Blewitt.*

THE BYE-LAWS

OF THE

ROCHE ✠ CRICKET ✠ CLUB.

1. That this Club shall be called "The Roche Cricket Club."

2. That any person be eligible for membership who is 16 years of age and over, but the Committee may elect any one who is younger at discretion.

3. Any person wishing to become a member is to signify the fact to the Secretary who shall bring his name before the Committee of the Club at their next meeting, and shall announce their decision to the applicant as soon as possible.

4. All questions relating to the election or dismissal of members shall be settled by the Committee.

5. The Committee shall consist of 8 members, and shall contain the President, Treasurer, Captain and Secretary of the Club as ex-officio Members, all of whom shall be elected annually.

6. Five members of the Committee shall constitute a quorum.

7. All questions at any meeting of the Committee shall be settled by a majority of votes the Chairman to have a casting vote in addition to his other vote.

8. The President, if present, shall take the chair at all meetings of the Club or Committee. In case of his absence, the Secretary shall take the chair until a chairman be elected by the meeting for the time being.

9. The Committee is to consist of :—

Rev. A. V. Thornton, President and Treasurer,
W. Robins, Captain,   A. H. Ham, Secretary,
W. J. Millett,   W. R. Goodfellow,
N. Robins,   F. Robins,
F. Bassett,   S. Brokenshile,
                F. Swainson,

with power to add to their number.

10. Any member of the Committee may call a meeting of the Committee by giving notice to the Secretary, who shall give at least 3 days' notice to the other members of the time and place of the meeting; but if the matter do not admit of delay a shorter notice will be sufficient. In the absence of the Secretary any officer of the Club will be competent to call a meeting.

11. A meeting of the whole Club shall be called by the Secretary at the order of the Committee, or on the written requisition of any 10 members of the Club.

12. At least 2 days' notice shall be given of a meeting of the whole Club

13. Any question to be decided by a majority of votes at any meeting of the whole Club, the Chairman to have a casting vote.

14. The Secretary is to give at least 3 days' notice of a match.

15. No member will be eligible to play in a match, unless he has played at least 6 times on the practice nights during the 3 weeks preceeding the match, except at the special request of the Committee.

16. Tuesdays, Thursdays, and Saturdays shall be the practice nights.

17. If the Captain be unable to be present on the practice nights he shall appoint a deputy for the night or forfeit 6d. to the funds of the Club.

18. Any member disobeying the command of the Captain or his deputy in the field, shall for the first offence be reprimanded by the Committee, for the second be fined 6d., and for the third be liable to dismissal from the Club, or to any other punishment the Committee may like to inflict.

19. Any member who uses blasphemous or indecent language or swears in the field shall be fined 6d.

20. Any member feeling himself aggrieved may appeal to a meeting of the Club, whose decision shall be final, provided 2 days' notice of the meeting has been given.

21. The Captain shall place the fieldsmen and appoint bowlers and batsmen at his discretion on practice nights as well as in matches; and shall endeavour to change the bowlers after every 4th over, with the object of giving every one present a chance of bowling on practice nights.

22. The subscriptions to the Club shall be fixed annually.

23. If any difficulty arise as to the interpretation of these rules, the decision of the Committee shall be final.

Dated July, 1886.

Above: The cricket team taken with the Rock in the background on 14th July, 1962.

Back row: *Penna (Umpire), Russell Hopper, Bernard Maycock, Eric Maycock, Gerald Smale, Mike Bowden, Ivor Yelland.*
Front row: *Ivor Penna, Anthony George, Rupert George, Ron Broom, Vivian Thomas.*

Below: Roche Old Boys' Cricket Team taken after a play off against St. Blazey on 22nd July, 1972.

Back row: *Rupert George, Christopher Trudgeon, Anthony George, Kevin Searle, Alastair Trudgeon, Mike Tregaskas, Roger Hawken, Norman Aspinwall.*
Front row: *David Trudgeon, Stevie Mills, Nigel Vivian, Ron Broom, Glyn Yelland.*

Top: This lovely postcard has a caption, *Man and Horse - Age 108 years*.
The photograph was taken on the corner of Harmony Road looking towards the Temperance Hotel.
Below: Procession ready for a carnival at Roche. Mr. Jimmy Grigg is seated, posing as the Mayor of Tregoss. This photograph was taken at Tregoss Farm.

Above: Postmen and ladies ready for delivery, standing outside the Post Office when it was in Harmony Road.

Left to right: *Mr. Jolly, Mr. Sherman, Mr. & Mrs. Clark (Postmaster), Mrs. Bassett, nee Dyer and Charles Hockley.*

Below: Looking up Harmony Road towards Tregoss. The Post Office can be seen on the end of the Terrace with the Blacksmith's Shop on the far end.

These photographs show Harmony Road council houses under construction in the early 1920's with the tradesmen and their tools. My father, Ralph Edyvean, is the boy standing on the bottom right in the lower photograph.

Above: Highertown Farm at around 1910-1912. The traction engine belonged to Mr. Hawkey of Trerank.

Below: An advertisement for Hadfield's Manure with Mr. Robert Cock from Bryn Farm.

Mr. ROBERT COCK, Bryn, Roche, says:—"I used your Manure 6 cwt. to the acre without farmyard, and am well pleased with it. The crop grew exceedingly well and weighed 75 tons per acre. For feeding, size and weight I have never had equal.

These photographs were both taken at Trerank Farm. Even the children turned out to help with the harvest.

Above: The mill wheel at Tregoss with Russell Edyvean standing and Alf Oliver sitting on the spokes.

Below: The Common family taken outside the Mill House at Tregoss. An old millstone was set into the door step.

These photographs show the quarry men and the Bal Maidens of Polpuff Glass Mine believed to have been taken about 1918. This is possibly the last large group of Bal Maidens in Cornwall.

This photograph shows the inside of the building at Beacon Clay Works. This was a German firm registered in 1912 which traded under the name of Standardized China Clay Co. A Mr. Gee patented a centrifuge processing system and this device was tried out at this works. This firm called in the Receivers on 9th May, 1924. During the First World War it was rumoured that German spies worked there.

The shell of the building can still be seen on the road between Goss Moor and Tregonetha.

This photograph shows the motor bucket dredger at Goss Moor. It was built by Werf Conrad on the side of one of the pools and then launched. The christening ceremony was performed by the wife, Mrs. Clark whose husband was the chairman of the British Alluvial Tin Syndicate Ltd., who leased the contract to work tin. It was named *Number One* and was launched into 20ft. of water. This was the first time that such a machine had been used. Before, it was worked by gravel pump system which was not entirely successful because of the working difficulties of clay soil interfering with the pumps. The company had a 21 year lease for 1,000 acres from Viscount Falmouth. The dredger cost £15,500 to build and weighed approximately 200 tons. It worked to a depth of 20ft. and had 40 buckets. It was fitted with four engines, two for working the processing equipment, one for reserve, the fourth for the generator. The dredger was 80ft. long and 35ft. wide. It was intended to employ about 50 men, and launched on 20th April, 1925. Tin was worked before the first World War from 1910-1912 by gravel pumps. Two companies tried without success.
Glass (Pyrolusite) found in Goss Moor in 1754.

Below: Photograph taken from the road showing the sand tip of North Goonbarrow Pit.

Above: Shows the North Goonbarrow Pit and the old Cornish beam engine houses which were used for pumping.

Below: This photograph was taken from the Tregonetha Road by Ellis of Bodmin on 30th October, 1939. There are a lot less sand tips on the horizon and a steam train is just about to cross Girder Bridge on the Newquay to Par Branch Line. The corn ricks are all thatched to keep them dry for threshing.
Photograph from Cornish Studies Library, Redruth Collection.

Newspaper Reports and Interesting Snippets

16th September, 1948
Adders at Roche
Adders seen to plentiful in the Roche district this year. Recently one 15inches long was killed on the Station and another was also seen, but got away before it could be caught. A third was killed at Demelza, a fourth was discovered in a cottage between Roche and Enniscaven. A Mr. Davy, puzzled as to why his wireless set refused to work, looked in at the back of it and found an adder coiled up. A neighbour facetiously suggested that it might have been attracted by the Third Programme.

3rd November, 1927
Roche Playing Field
This was a gift to the people of Roche from a Mr. A. Bennetts. He left Roche in 1880 and returned a successful man. The playing field was given by him in return for the kindness he received from the people of Roche. The ceremony took place in the school because of heavy rain. The gate was opened by The Lord Lieutenant of Cornwall, Mr. J.C. Williams, and the bells rung from the church. The service was conducted by Rev. J. Tarplee.

17th April, 1925.
Gold Discoveries
Gold has been found in a number of localities in the county. Early Cornish historians mentioned the fact that tinners working on alluvial tin in the Goss Moors collected native gold in quills which they sold for their personal benefit.

The Reverend Fisher's furniture was sold in 1834 for the sum of 7s. 6d. (37½p.)

During the time that Parson Lowe was Rector of Roche (1903-1921) there was an annual Rook Shoot at the Rectory after nesting time.